Nifty Thrifty Crafts for Kids

Nifty Thrifty ART Crafts

Heather Miller

Enslow Elementary

an imprint of

Enslow Publishers, Inc.

40 Industrial Road
Box 398
Berkeley Heights, NJ 07922
USA

http://www.enslow.com

Enslow Elementary, an imprint of Enslow Publishers, Inc.

Enslow Elementary® is a registered trademark of Enslow Publishers, Inc.

Library of Congress Cataloging-in-Publication Data

Miller, Heather.

  Nifty thrifty crafts for kids. Nifty thrifty art crafts / Heather Miller. — 1st ed.

    p. cm.

  Includes bibliographical references and index.

  ISBN-13: 978-0-7660-2780-0

  ISBN-10: 0-7660-2780-5

    1. Handicraft—Juvenile literature. 2. Recycling (Waste, etc.)—Juvenile literature.

  I. Title. II. Title: Nifty thrifty art crafts.

  TT160.M477 2007

  745.5—dc22

                              2006018293

Printed in the United States of America

10 9 8 7 6 5 4 3 2

To Our Readers: We have done our best to make sure all Internet Addresses in this book were active and appropriate when we went to press. However, the author and the publisher have no control over and assume no liability for the material available on those Internet sites or on other Web sites they may link to. Any comments or suggestions can be sent by e-mail to comments@enslow.com or to the address on the back cover.

Every effort has been made to locate all copyright holders of material used in this book. If any errors or omissions have occurred, corrections will be made in future editions of this book.

Illustration Credits: Crafts prepared by June Ponte; photography by Nicole diMella/Enslow Publishers, Inc.; Hemera Technologies, Inc. 1997–2000, pp. 2, 30, 31, 32; AP, p. 27 (Warhol); Corel Corporation, p. 26 ("Stag and Reindeer" and hieroglyphics), 27 (Seurat); Courtesy of Government Printing Office, Republic of China, p. 26 (Ancient Chinese Paper); © 2007 Jupiterimages Corporation, p. 26 (Hokusai); Shutterstock, p. 27 (Indian Princess); Wikipedia, p. 27 (Pollock and Calder).

Cover Illustration: Photography by Nicole diMella/Enslow Publishers, Inc.

Safety Note: Be sure to ask for help from an adult, if needed, to complete these crafts!

Contents

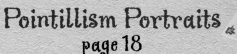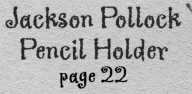

Introduction

Many objects we normally toss into the trash can be turned into exciting works of art.

Your house is probably filled with supplies you can use to create fun and unusual works of art. You may start looking at everyday trash in a new way. Clean up a foam meat tray and use it to create a simple printing press. Use cotton swabs to paint a picture of yourself! Start collecting bits of this and pieces of that. What you once thought was trash, may now be a treasure.

Making something new out of something old is not a new idea. Ancient people used charred scraps of wood and ground minerals to decorate the walls of caves. Chinese inventors chopped and pounded plant fibers to create the first sheets of paper. American Indians used materials from plants and animals to create clothing and pouches. Even modern artists like Andy Warhol used common objects, such as soup cans, as inspiration for their great works.

Artists are problem solvers that take ordinary things and transform them. The next time you are about to throw something away, think about it—it could be a work of art!

We talk about many different types of art and artists in this book. To see real-life examples, please go to page 26 for "What It Really Looks Like."

Egyptian Hieroglyphs

5

Cave Painting Placemats

Are You Ready?

Over sixty years ago, three boys made an incredible discovery in the French countryside. Just outside the village of Montignac, the boys crawled into a hole in the ground left by a fallen tree. Inside they discovered cave paintings left by ancient people. Created with materials such as charcoal and animal fats, the art found on the walls of Lascaux Cave is both beautiful and mysterious. Use modern materials to create your own cave paintings.

Get Set

- ✔ brown paper bag
- ✔ crayons
- ✔ paper bowl
- ✔ measuring cup
- ✔ teaspoon
- ✔ water
- ✔ black poster paint
- ✔ paintbrush
- ✔ newspapers
- ✔ paper towels
- ✔ construction paper
- ✔ white glue

Let's Go!

1. Tear a section from a brown paper bag. The ragged edges will give the paper a prehistoric look.

2. Using crayons, create your own prehistoric design.

3. Crumple your drawing and squeeze it gently under running water. Carefully open the paper to reveal a web of wrinkles. Let dry.

6

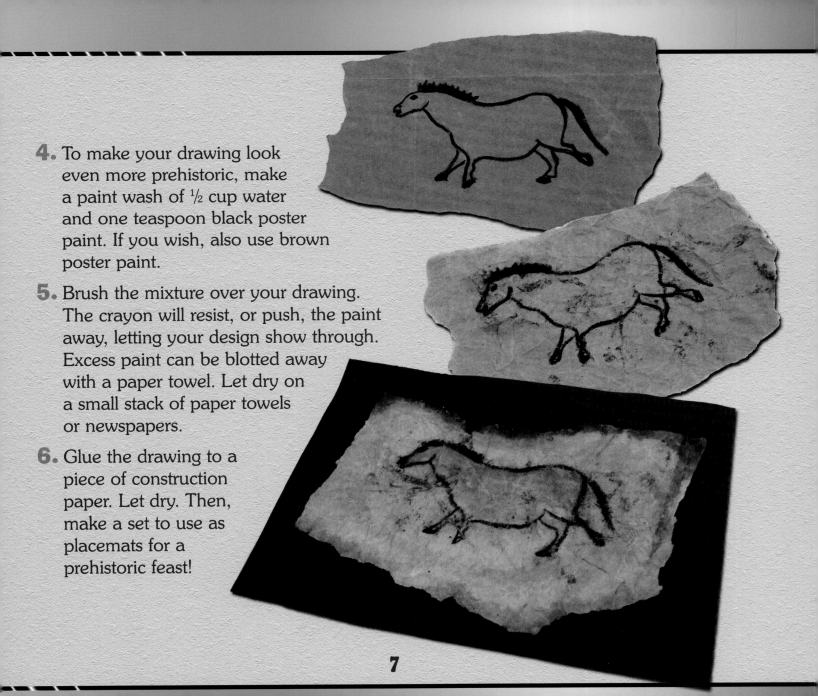

4. To make your drawing look even more prehistoric, make a paint wash of ½ cup water and one teaspoon black poster paint. If you wish, also use brown poster paint.

5. Brush the mixture over your drawing. The crayon will resist, or push, the paint away, letting your design show through. Excess paint can be blotted away with a paper towel. Let dry on a small stack of paper towels or newspapers.

6. Glue the drawing to a piece of construction paper. Let dry. Then, make a set to use as placemats for a prehistoric feast!

Hieroglyphic Symbols

Ancient Egyptians developed a unique form of writing. Small pictures and symbols called hieroglyphs were used to represent sounds. Combinations of these symbols were made to create words. Just like the English alphabet, endless combinations of these symbols could be made to represent thousands of words. But, unlike the English alphabet, Egyptian hieroglyphs are pictures and are therefore meant to be beautiful. You can share the ideas of ancient Egyptians and create a symbol that represents the beauty inside yourself!

Get Set

- ✔ pencil
- ✔ sketch paper
- ✔ white paper
- ✔ aluminum foil
- ✔ old magazine or newspapers
- ✔ crayon
- ✔ scissors
- ✔ an empty cereal box
- ✔ clear tape
- ✔ pipe cleaners

Let's Go!

1. Begin by writing a list of words that describe you. Use the words as an inspiration for your personal symbol. Spend some time sketching ideas. Once you decide on a symbol, draw it carefully on a clean sheet of paper. (For the symbol shown, see page 30.)

HAPPY
FUNNY
SMART
SILLY

8

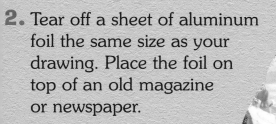

2. Tear off a sheet of aluminum foil the same size as your drawing. Place the foil on top of an old magazine or newspaper.

3. Lay your drawing on top of the foil. Draw over your design with a crayon or pencil. Do not press too hard, or you will break through the foil.

4. Remove the paper. Turn the foil over to reveal your design.

5. Leave a 1-inch border around your design. Cut off the rest of the foil. Cut a piece of light cardboard a little smaller than your foil design. Wrap the foil around the cardboard. If needed, use clear tape to tape the foil to the cardboard.

6. Tape pipe cleaners to the back of the cardboard around the outside. Bend each pipe cleaner into an interesting shape. Display on your bedroom door or wall.

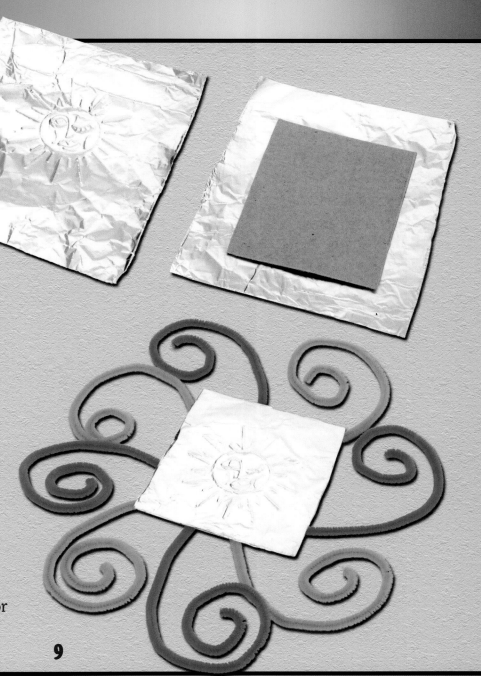

Sandpaper Pyramid Paperweight

Are You Ready?

The image of a pyramid is often used to represent mystery and the unknown. There are many mysteries connected to the pyramids of Giza in Egypt. Historians still debate basic questions concerning how old the pyramids are, how they were built, and how many men and women worked to complete their construction. Some historians theorize that it took twenty thousand to thirty thousand workers over eighty years to build the pyramids of Giza. Build your own mysterious pyramid miniature in just one afternoon.

Get Set

- ✔ **paper**
- ✔ **pencil**
- ✔ **ruler**
- ✔ **scissors**
- ✔ **crayons or markers**
- ✔ **an empty cereal box**
- ✔ **a small rock**
- ✔ **clear tape**
- ✔ **tacky craft glue**
- ✔ **sandpaper**

Let's Go!

1. Draw a triangle on paper with all three sides measuring 3 inches (see A). (See page 28 for the pattern.)

2. Use the paper triangle as a pattern to trace four triangles onto the smooth side of sandpaper. Cut them out (see B).

3. Using crayons or markers, decorate the rough side of each triangle with Egyptian symbols (see C). (See page 30 for some symbols, or make your own.)

A

B

4. Use the paper triangle to trace four triangles onto the cardboard. Cut them out.

5. Tape a small rock to one of the cardboard triangles (see D). This is the base of the pyramid.

6. Place the other cardboard triangles around the base. Secure them to the base with clear tape. If you wish, before you seal the pyramid closed, write a secret or a wish on a small piece of paper. Tuck the paper inside your pyramid.

7. Fold up the triangle around the base (see E). Tape them together.

8. Use tacky craft glue to glue the decorative sandpaper triangles to the outside of the cardboard pyramid (see F). Let dry. (White glue will melt the sandpaper.)

9. Make several pyramids, and display them together to create your own Egyptian desert.

Chinese Papermaking Window Decorations

Tearing, pounding, mixing, and pouring. These are some of the steps involved in making paper. The Chinese are credited with the invention of paper, and it is thought that the earliest sheets of paper were made from hemp, tree bark, and bamboo. Most historians agree that Ts'ai Lun was the first to bring the invention of paper to the attention of the emperor in A.D. 105. Even though the creation of paper is an ancient art, many people still enjoy the process today. Give it a try with this interesting paper recycling project.

Get Set

- ✔ old newspapers
- ✔ scissors
- ✔ large bowl
- ✔ measuring cup
- ✔ water
- ✔ food coloring
- ✔ wooden spoon
- ✔ can opener
- ✔ two empty tin cans, close to the same size
- ✔ small scrap of window screen, burlap, or plastic canvas (Ask permission first!)
- ✔ shallow pan or plastic tray
- ✔ glitter (optional)
- ✔ paper towels
- ✔ hole punch
- ✔ string or yarn

Let's Go!

1. Tear or cut one sheet of newspaper into tiny pieces, about the size of small coins (see A).

2. Put the small pieces of newspaper into a large bowl and cover with about 4 cups of warm water. Be sure all the paper is soaked in water. You may need to add more water later since the paper will absorb it quickly.

3. Add several drops of food coloring to the mixture and stir. Let the paper mixture sit for a few hours. It is done when it is nice and mushy.

4. Ask an adult to help you remove both ends from two empty cans (see B). (Each can should be open like a tube.)

A

B

C

5. Cut a square of window screen, burlap, or plastic canvas just large enough to cover the top of one can.

6. Place one can inside the shallow pan or plastic tray. Set the screen on top of the can. Stack the second can on top of the screen (see C).

7. Scoop ¼ cup of the paper pulp out of the bowl and carefully pour it into the top can. If you wish, sprinkle the pulp with glitter.

8. Wait for most of the water to drain (see D). Carefully lift away the top can.

9. Place a small sheet of folded newspaper or paper towel over the paper circle. Press gently to remove more water.

10. Lift the newspaper and paper circle from the screen and can. Set it in a safe place to dry. Once dry, carefully peel the paper circle from the newspaper.

11. Carefully punch a hole in the top. Thread with string or yarn and hang in a window (see E).

D

E

Japanese Relief Print Journal Cover

Are You Ready?

While the Chinese may have been the first to develop the basic form of printmaking, the Japanese turned the method into an art form. The print artist, Katsushika Hokusai created over 35,000 prints and drawings during the late 17th and early 18th centuries. Hokusai used a method called relief printing to create his works. To create a relief print, the artist first carves an image into a soft surface such as wood, linoleum, or foam. Ink is applied to the surface of the carved plate and the image is then pressed onto paper. Printed images may be made over and over again.

Get Set

- ✔ **construction paper**
- ✔ **notebook (optional)**
- ✔ **scissors**
- ✔ **foam meat or cheese tray, washed and dried**
- ✔ **dull pencil**
- ✔ **paintbrush**
- ✔ **poster paint**
- ✔ **white glue**

Let's Go!

1. Sketch a design on a piece of construction paper that is the same size as your journal cover (see A). (See page 29 for the pattern.) If you do not have a journal, use an old or new notebook.

2. Cut the sides off a foam tray to make one flat piece.

3. Place the sketched design on the smooth side of the foam. Use a dull pencil to press firmly as you draw over the design. The pencil should leave an imprint of your design in the foam (see B).

A

4. Apply an even layer of poster paint over the design (see C). Turn the tray over, paint side down, onto a new piece of construction paper. Press firmly with the palms of both hands.

5. Carefully peel the paper away to reveal the design. Let dry.

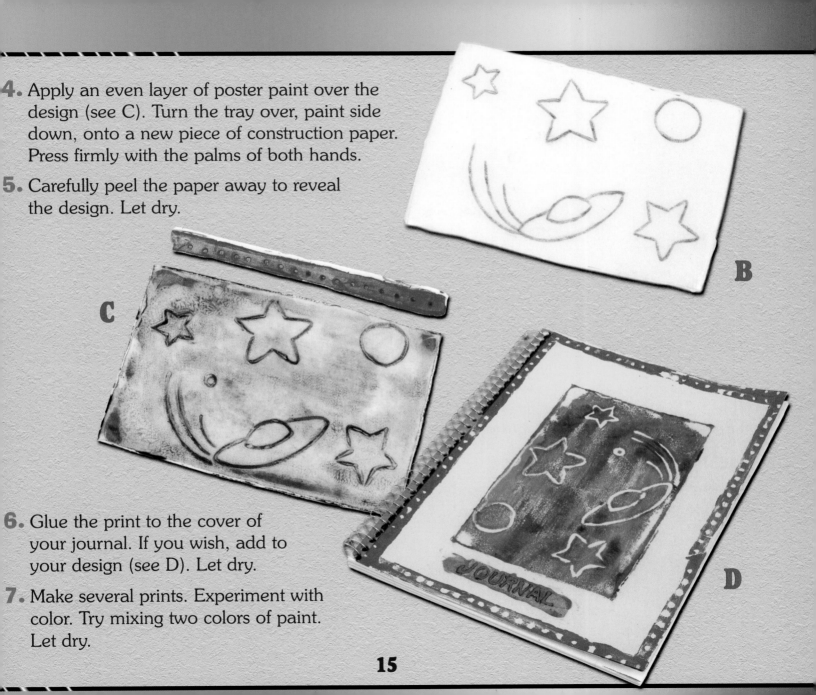

B

C

6. Glue the print to the cover of your journal. If you wish, add to your design (see D). Let dry.

7. Make several prints. Experiment with color. Try mixing two colors of paint. Let dry.

D

American Indian Textured Pouch

European clothing included sewn pockets, but American Indians made small pouches to carry important items such as food, beads, tools, medicine, and fire-starters. Made from animal skins, pouches both large and small were carried by American Indian men, women, and children. Use the following directions to create your own pouch, then use it to collect interesting finds on your next nature hike.

Get Set

- ✔ scissors
- ✔ an empty cereal box
- ✔ poster paint (optional)
- ✔ paintbrush (optional)
- ✔ ruler
- ✔ pencil
- ✔ hole punch
- ✔ yarn
- ✔ old shoelaces (optional)
- ✔ white glue
- ✔ leaves, seeds, grass, beads
- ✔ zipper top bag

Let's Go!

1. Cut one large side from an empty cereal box. Fold the cardboard in half so the inside shows (see A). Unfold. If you wish, use poster paint to paint the inside of the cardboard. Let dry.

2. With a pencil and ruler, make 5 to 6 "x" marks on two short sides. Make them evenly spaced. Fold the cardboard. Make "x" marks on the other two short sides so the marks line up. Use a hole punch to carefully punch out the "x" marks. The holes should match up when the cardboard is folded. Make sure the plain or painted side is showing (see B).

3. Cut a piece of yarn about 24 inches. With the cardboard folded, thread the yarn through the bottom holes of one short side of the cardboard. Tie a knot. Weave the yarn through the holes until you get to the top. Tie a knot. Cut off any extra yarn. Do the same thing to the other side (see C).

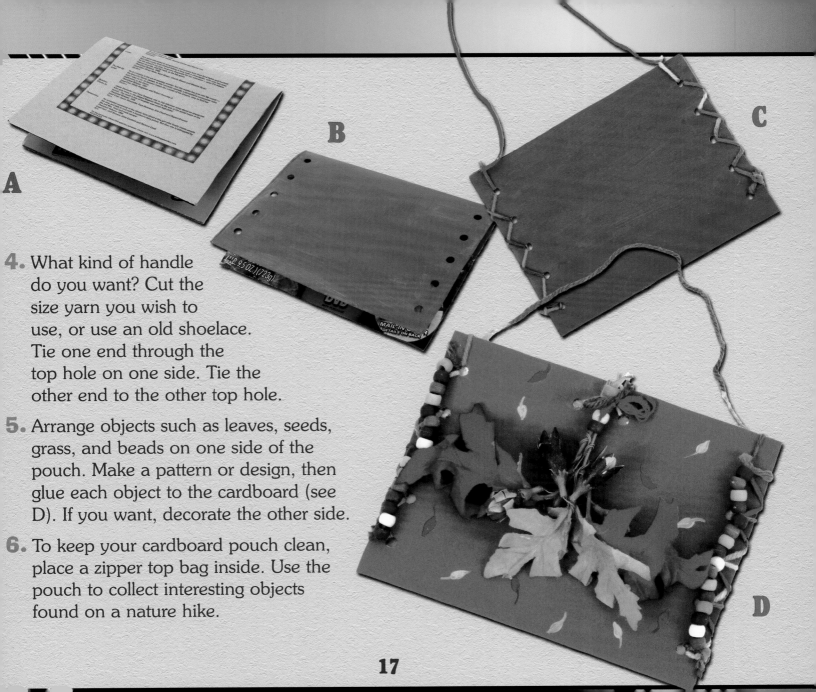

A

B

C

4. What kind of handle do you want? Cut the size yarn you wish to use, or use an old shoelace. Tie one end through the top hole on one side. Tie the other end to the other top hole.

5. Arrange objects such as leaves, seeds, grass, and beads on one side of the pouch. Make a pattern or design, then glue each object to the cardboard (see D). If you want, decorate the other side.

6. To keep your cardboard pouch clean, place a zipper top bag inside. Use the pouch to collect interesting objects found on a nature hike.

D

Pointillism Portraits

Are You Ready?

Georges-Pierre Seurat (1859–1891) developed a style of painting called pointillism. Pointillism is the process of painting with short brush strokes, or dots. When looked at from a distance, the brushstrokes in a pointillism painting blend together, creating one whole, smooth image. Use Seurat's method of dot painting to create an unusual portrait of yourself.

Get Set

- ✔ **mirror**
- ✔ **pencil**
- ✔ **construction paper**
- ✔ **cotton swabs**
- ✔ **poster paint**

Let's Go!

1. Set up your work space in front of a mirror. Study your face carefully.

2. Use a pencil to draw a simple portrait on construction paper. Do not worry if it turns out looking a bit funny. It is art!

18

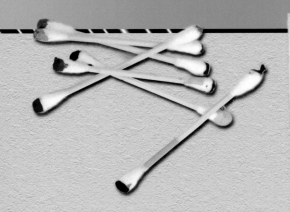

3. Dip the end of a cotton swab into poster paint. Fill in the portrait by stamping small dots with the cotton swab.

4. Use different colors to add more feeling to your portrait. Let dry.

5. What does your portrait look like up-close? What does it look like from far away?

Pop Art Stamp

Are You Ready?

Andy Warhol (1928–1987) was one of the most influential American artists in recent history. Two of his favorite methods of creating art were photography and silkscreen printing. Warhol used common things, like soup cans, as inspiration for his paintings. Try this project that uses common objects found in your home to create your own piece of pop art.

Get Set

✔ marker

✔ new, clean kitchen sponge

✔ scissors

✔ ruler

✔ pencil

✔ construction paper

✔ poster paint

Let's Go!

1. Decide on a simple shape such as a star, heart, circle, or triangle. (See page 28 for a heart pattern.) With a marker, draw the shape onto a new, clean kitchen sponge. Cut it out (see A).

2. Draw a grid on construction paper with a pencil and ruler so there are six spaces on the paper. Go over the lines with a marker (see B).

3. Choose six different colors of poster paint.

4. Dip the sponge into one color and stamp onto one space on the construction paper. Rinse the sponge. Make sure to wring out the water well. Dip the sponge into another color and stamp onto another space. Repeat this process until each space has a different color stamped shape (see C). Let dry.

5. Make more "pop art" with other shapes and other objects.

A

B

C

21

Jackson Pollock Pencil Holder

Are You Ready?

Instead of creating careful drawings and designs, Jackson Pollock (1912–1956) splashed, dribbled, and threw paints onto his canvases. While most painters place their canvases on an easel, Pollock laid his out on the floor. There he could walk around, and sometimes step onto, the painting while he splattered colors this way and that. The finished paintings brought forth feelings of excitement and energy, a true reflection of Pollock's unusual painting style.

Get Set

- ✔ newspaper
- ✔ paper bowls
- ✔ poster paint
- ✔ white glue
- ✔ craft sticks
- ✔ white construction paper
- ✔ old toothbrush (Get permission first!)
- ✔ empty soup can, washed and dried
- ✔ ruler
- ✔ pencil
- ✔ scissors

Let's Go!

1. Cover your workspace with newspaper.

2. Choose four different poster paint colors. Pour small amounts of each color into separate paper bowls. Pour about twice that amount of white glue into each paper bowl. Use craft sticks to stir the paint and glue mixture.

3. Place a piece of white construction paper on the newspapers in front of you. Dip an old toothbrush into one color. Lightly tap the top of the toothbrush, bristles side down, over the paper. Rinse the toothbrush off before going to the next color. Repeat the process for each color. Let dry.

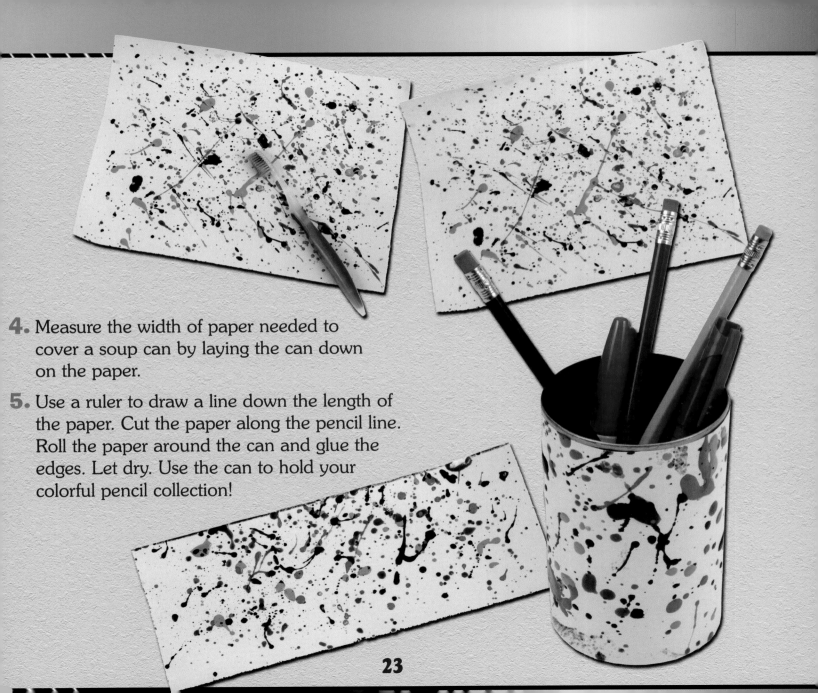

4. Measure the width of paper needed to cover a soup can by laying the can down on the paper.

5. Use a ruler to draw a line down the length of the paper. Cut the paper along the pencil line. Roll the paper around the can and glue the edges. Let dry. Use the can to hold your colorful pencil collection!

Calder CD Mobile

Are You Ready?

Alexander Calder (1898–1976) was one of the first to create moveable sculptures in the form of mobiles. Mobiles are sculptures that combine shape with movement and balance. Calder used materials such as wire and metal to create both very large and very small mobiles. He enjoyed using bright colors and simple shapes to compose his designs. You can use the simple shape of a circle to create your own mobile from old computer CDs.

Get Set

- ✔ wire clothes hanger
- ✔ ruler
- ✔ string
- ✔ scissors
- ✔ 5 old computer CDs (Ask permission first!)
- ✔ glitter (optional)
- ✔ beads (optional)
- ✔ white glue
- ✔ permanent markers
- ✔ paintbrush
- ✔ poster paint
- ✔ light cardboard
- ✔ aluminum foil

Let's Go!

1. Use the hanger as a foundation for the mobile (see A).

2. Cut nine pieces of string of different lengths (ranging from 6 inches to 18 inches) and set aside.

3. Decorate five CDs with permanent markers, glitter, and beads. Let dry. Thread a piece of string through the center hole of each CD and tie (see B).

4. Cut cardboard into four interesting shapes. Tape one end of a piece of string to the back of each cardboard piece. Cover each shape with aluminum foil, leaving the rest of the string out. If you wish, use poster paint to decorate the foil shapes (see B). Let dry.

5. Tie the other end of all nine strings to the hanger. Try to balance your mobile so it will hang and move smoothly (see C).

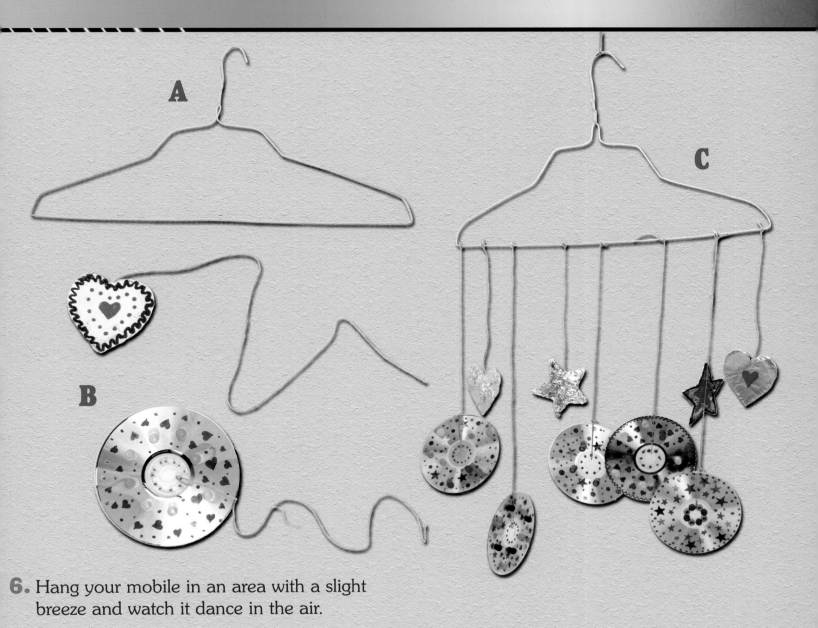

6. Hang your mobile in an area with a slight breeze and watch it dance in the air.

What It Really Looks Like

Have you wondered what a cave drawing really looks like? How about a relief print or a mobile? Here are "real" inspirations of what you created in this book.

**"Stag and Reindeer"
Lascaux, Dordogne, France.**
Cave Painting Placemats, page 6

Egyptian Hieroglyphics
Hieroglyphic Symbols, page 8

Pyramids. Cairo, Egypt
Sandpaper Pyramid Paperweight, page 10

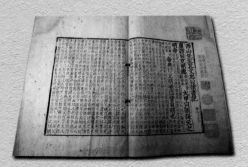

Ancient Chinese Paper
Chinese Papermaking Window Decorations, page 12

"The Wave" by Hokusai
Japanese Relief Print Journal Cover, page 14

Indian Princess
at a
Minneapolis
PowWow
**American Indian
Textured Pouch,
page 16**

"Bathers at Asnières" by Georges Seurat
Pointillism Portraits, page 18

"One: Number 31, 1950" by Jackson Pollock
Jackson Pollock Pencil Holder, page 22

Screen print series of Marilyn Monroe
from 1967 by Andy Warhol
Pop Art Stamp, page 20

"Red Mobile" by Alexander Calder
Calder CD Mobile, page 24

Patterns

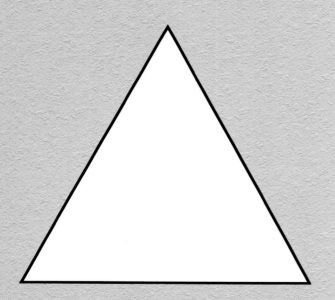

Sandpaper Pyramid Paperweight
at 100%

Pop Art Stamp
at 100%

Japanese Relief Print Journal Cover at 100%

sun

quail chick

foot

basket with handle

owl

water

horned viper

door bolt

hand

Hieroglyphic Symbols at 100%

Reading About

Books

Ancona, George. *Murals: Walls That Sing.* New York: Marshall Cavendish, 2003.

Bennett, Leonie. *Jackson Pollock.* Chicago, Ill.: Heinemann Library, 2005.

Mattern, Joanne. *Andy Warhol.* Edina, Minn.: Abdo Pub., 2005.

Schaefer, Adam. *Alexander Calder.* Chicago, Ill.: Heinemann Library, 2003.

Venezia, Mike. *Georges Seurat.* New York: Children's Press, 2002.

Internet Addresses

Hieroglyphs: Writing
<http://www.greatscott.com/hiero/hiero_alpha.html>
This Web site gives more examples of hieroglyphic symbols.

Crafts for Kids
<http://crafts.kaboose.ca>
Go to this site for more fun crafts!

Index